GROUND BREAKERS
BLACK MOVIE MAKERS

MELVIN AND MARIO VAN PEEBLES

by Joyce Markovics
and Alrick A. Brown

Cherry Lake Press
cherrylakepublishing.com

Cherry Lake Press

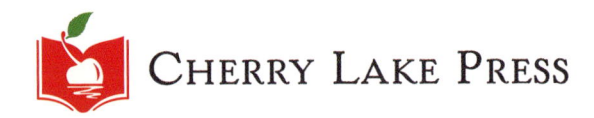

Published in the United States of America by Cherry Lake Publishing Group
Ann Arbor, Michigan
www.cherrylakepublishing.com

Reading Adviser: Beth Walker Gambro, MS, Ed., Reading Consultant, Yorkville, IL
Content Adviser: Alrick A. Brown, Film Professor and Filmmaker
Book Designer: Ed Morgan

Photo Credits: © Fitzroy Barrett/ZUMAPRESS/Newscom, cover and title page; © John Barrett/ZUMAPRESS/Newscom, 5; Public Domain, 6; freepik.com, 7; Wikimedia Commons, 8; freepik.com, 9; Wikimedia Commons, 10; © Keystone Press/Alamy Stock Photo, 11; freepik.com, 12; © COLUMBIA PICTURES/Ronald Grant Archive/Alamy Stock Photo, 13; Wikimedia Commons, 14; © Kathy Hutchins/Shutterstock, 15; © Kraft74/Shutterstock, 16; © WARNER BROTHERS/Album/Newscom, 17; © Michael Sherer/Polaris/Newscom, 18; © Alrick A. Brown, 19; © KATHY HUTCHINS/Kathy Hutchins Photography/Newscom, 21.

Copyright © 2023 by Cherry Lake Publishing Group

Cherry Lake Press is an imprint of Cherry Lake Publishing Group.

All rights reserved. No part of this book may be reproduced or utilized in any form or by any means without written permission from the publisher.

Library of Congress Cataloging-in-Publication Data has been filed and is available at catalog.loc.gov.

Printed in the United States of America by
Corporate Graphics

CONTENTS

This Is Melvin and Mario ... 4
Early Life 6
Making Movies 12
Impact 20

Filmography 22
Glossary 23
Find Out More 24
Index 24
About the Authors 24

THIS IS MELVIN AND MARIO

> "MY DAD DIDN'T OPEN DOORS, HE BLEW THEM UP."
> —MARIO VAN PEEBLES

Father and son filmmakers Melvin and Mario Van Peebles changed cinema in a big way. Melvin made **independent** movies that **empowered** Black people from all walks of life. No one before him had done that. With a bold and direct style, he forced people to think and act. Melvin also **mentored** other groundbreaking Black directors, including his own son, Mario. Today, Mario proudly carries his father's **legacy**.

Melvin and Mario Van Peebles, father and son filmmakers

Melvin Van Peebles was more than a filmmaker. He was also a painter, author, songwriter, actor, pilot, and the first Black Wall Street trader, among other things!

EARLY LIFE

> "HE WORE GLASSES, AND HE LOOKED KIND OF GEEKY, REALLY."
> —MARY MCCALL, MELVIN'S CHILDHOOD FRIEND

Melvin Peebles was born on August 21, 1932. He was raised on the South Side of Chicago by parents Edwin Griffin and Marion Peebles. Edwin worked as a tailor. The family had little money. To help out, Melvin sold used clothes from his dad's tailor shop on the street.

The South Side of Chicago, Illinois, in the 1940s, where Melvin grew up

In school, young Melvin loved art and was one of the brightest students. Yet he was also bullied for being small and awkward. To escape his bullies, he retreated to the library. Melvin attended high school in Phoenix, Illinois, where he was one of the only Black kids. Melvin **excelled** there too and got a **scholarship** to college.

As a child, Melvin enjoyed reading and writing. He went on to write several books as an adult.

In high school, Melvin wore orange shoes that squeaked as he walked. "It was real amusing to everybody," said his friend Mary McCall.

7

> "I STARTED LIFE AS A PAINTER AND SCULPTOR."
> —MELVIN VAN PEEBLES

For college, Melvin went to Ohio Wesleyan to study art and literature. "To get enough money to finish college, I joined the ROTC," he said. At age 20, 13 days after graduation, Melvin became an officer in the U.S. Air Force. He served for a little over 3 years navigating planes. In 1956, Melvin met and married a German actress and artist named Maria Marx. They moved to Mexico and had two children, Mario and Megan. Melvin worked as a portrait painter to support his family. In 1957, Melvin and his family went to San Francisco to live.

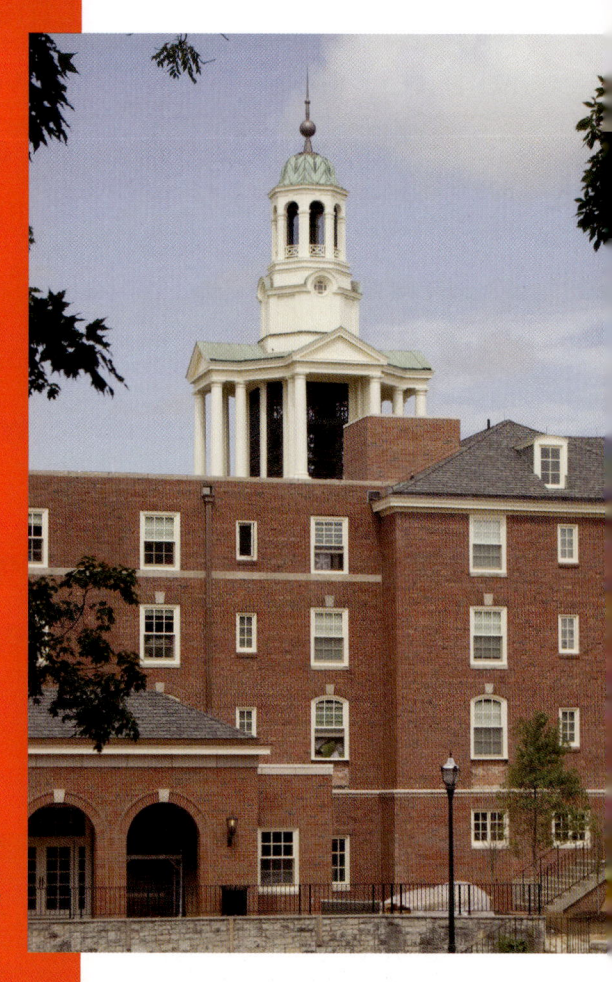

Ohio Wesleyan University in Delaware, Ohio

The Golden Gate Bridge in San Francisco, California

Later in his life, Melvin had two other children. Their names are Max and Marguerite. All of Melvin's kids have names that begin with the letter *M*.

In San Francisco, Melvin worked as a cable car driver. He wrote a book called *The Big Heart* in 1957 about his experiences. A passenger suggested that Melvin make movies. When Melvin's boss found out about the book and that Melvin could read, he fired him.

A cable car on Hyde Street in San Francisco, California

"ALL I EVER WANTED TO DO WAS TELL STORIES."
—MELVIN VAN PEEBLES

Determined to make movies, Melvin taught himself how. He started with short **experimental** films. With his films in hand, Melvin went to Hollywood to find a job. When the only one he could find was as an elevator operator, Melvin packed up his family and moved to the Netherlands. Not long after, he separated from Maria and moved to Paris, France.

This is Melvin in 1967. He added "Van" to his name when he moved to the Netherlands.

In the Netherlands, Melvin studied **astronomy**. He became interested in astronomy as a navigator. "Sometimes you're not able to use the equipment, so you'd have to do it the old-fashioned way, figuring out what you were seeing in the sky."

11

MAKING MOVIES

Melvin taught himself how to speak French and sang on the streets for money. He kept writing and eventually got his work published in a French magazine. Melvin turned one of his stories into a 1967 **feature film** called *The Story of a Three-Day Pass*. It's about a Black soldier who's attacked for having a white girlfriend. The movie won a **Critics**' Choice Award.

> "I DO WHAT I WANT TO DO."
> —MELVIN VAN PEEBLES

Doors began opening for Melvin. A Hollywood movie studio hired him to direct *Watermelon Man* in 1970. The story follows a **racist** white man who wakes up one morning as a Black man. The movie was a box-office success. The studio wanted Melvin to change the ending, but he refused. Melvin was offered a multi-movie deal from the same studio. "That's every filmmaker's dream. But it wasn't mine," said Melvin. He knew he wouldn't have full control. So Melvin set out to make a movie on his own.

Melvin (right) with actor Godfrey Cambridge on the set of *Watermelon Man*

While living in Paris, Melvin learned that the French government funded the films of French writers. So, he wrote four books in French to get the money he needed to make his first film!

With only a small **budget**, Melvin worked nonstop to complete his second feature film. To save money, he used 13-year-old Mario and other family members as actors. And he cast himself as the lead character—a strong Black man who fights against racism and for what he thinks is right. The movie is raw, violent, and filled with **controversy**. It even has a controversial title. However, it showed the world as many Black Americans experienced it.

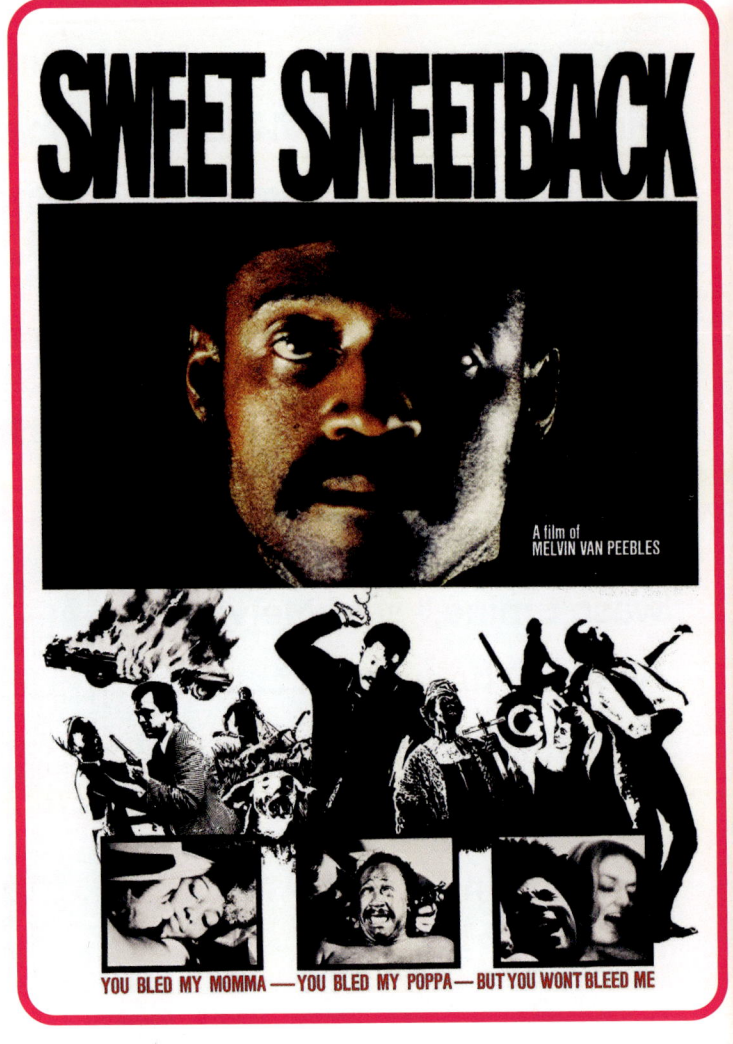

A poster for Melvin's second feature film

"IF YOU GIVE PEOPLE SOMETHING THEY WANT, THEY'LL COME AND SEE IT."
—MELVIN VAN PEEBLES

"I wanted a movie that Black people could walk out of standing proud," Melvin said. He wanted to make a movie about Black people *for* Black people. And Melvin did. Thousands of Black Americans turned out to see it. And the film became the highest-earning independent movie of 1971. It was "the first time an independent film made that kind of money and was that successful and taken seriously," said Melvin.

Melvin (center) with Mario (left) and Mario's son (right)

Mario spent a lot of time on the movie set. He learned a lot about filmmaking from his dad.

Two Blaxploitation movies that came out after Melvin's film were *Shaft* and *Super Fly*.

Melvin's film sparked a movement. More Black-made movies about strong Black characters followed. They were called Blaxploitation (blak-sploi-TEY-shuhn) films. Then Melvin turned his attention to other interests, including music. He focused on musical theater. Then in the mid-1980s, Melvin did something wildly different. He traded stocks on Wall Street! "Making deals, like always," he said.

Not all Black people supported Blaxploitation films. Some thought the movies pushed racist **stereotypes**.

Around this time, Mario was busy working as an actor. But he wanted to make movies like his dad. Mario directed his first movie, *New Jack City*, in 1991. It was a big hit. More followed. Melvin guided Mario along the way. "My father told me you have two loves in your life: what you do and the people you're with," said Mario.

A still image from *New Jack City* directed by Mario

"GREAT ALLIES COME IN ALL COLORS. THEY DON'T ALWAYS LOOK LIKE YOU, OR VOTE LIKE YOU."
—MARIO VAN PEEBLES

In 2003, Mario wrote and directed a movie about his dad. He even played him in it! The film paid **homage** to his father in a deeply personal way. It showed a loving and complex relationship. Critics named it one of the best films of the year. Melvin was especially proud of his son's work.

Melvin stands on the terrace of his NYC apartment. One of his favorite sayings was, "Keep on keepin' on."

Apart from Mario, Melvin mentored other young Black filmmakers, including Alrick Brown. Melvin became like a father to Alrick. Alrick learned about filmmaking from Melvin—and also about life. "I met Mr. Van Peebles when I was in graduate film school," said Alrick. "I learned more from him about storytelling and the film business than I learned in school." On top of Melvin's artistic genius, Alrick saw his mentor's big heart. "I loved him," Alrick said. "And I will never forget him."

Alrick Brown with Melvin, his mentor and beloved friend

"Some fathers will teach you how to play ball. I'm going to try to teach you how to own the team," Melvin once said.

IMPACT

> "I WANTED TO MAKE IT POSSIBLE FOR A NEW GENERATION TO MAKE FILMS."
> —MELVIN VAN PEEBLES

On September 21, 2021, Melvin Van Peebles passed away at age 89. He died in his apartment in New York City. Mario was by his side. Their relationship was close until the end. "Growing up with him, I saw a life well lived, fully lived," said Mario. One lesson he learned from his filmmaker father was to always try to make a difference. Melvin would say to his son, "Try to teach and mentor someone who doesn't always look like you . . . or think like you." Melvin pushed boundaries—and changed the film world forever. He is more than a groundbreaker. Melvin is a legend.

Here are Melvin and Mario in 2005. A devoted son and teacher, Mario continues to celebrate his father. For example, he's working to bring one of his dad's musicals back to Broadway.

Melvin danced to his own tune, literally. He wrote the music to many of his films.

FILMOGRAPHY

A SELECTION OF MELVIN AND MARIO'S FEATURE FILMS

Melvin Van Peebles

1967	*Story of a Three-Day Pass*
1970	*Watermelon Man*
1971	*Sweet Sweetback's . . . Song*
2000	*Bellyfull*

Mario Van Peebles

1991	*New Jack City*
1993	*Posse*
1995	*Panther*
2006	*Hard Luck*

GLOSSARY

astronomy (uh-STRON-uh-mee) the science of studying outer space

budget (BUHJ-it) an estimate of expected expenses for a given time

controversy (KON-truh-vur-see) a dispute concerning a matter of opinion

critics (KRIT-iks) people who judge or criticize something

empowered (em-POU-urd) gave something the power or authority to do something

excelled (ek-SELD) performed very well

experimental (ek-sper-uh-MEN-tuhl) relating to something cutting edge

feature film (FEE-chur FILM) a full-length movie

homage (HOM-ij) paid respect to

independent (in-di-PEN-duhnt) free from outside control

legacy (LEG-uh-see) anything handed down from the past

literature (LIT-er-uh-cher) written works

mentored (MEN-tawrd) advised, guided, or trained

navigating (NAV-uh-gayt-ing) finding one's way from place to place

racist (RAY-sist) someone who treats people unfairly or cruelly because of their race or ethnicity

ROTC (AHR-OH-TEE-SEE) stands for the Reserve Officers' Training Corps, a college program that prepares young adults to become officers in the U.S. military

scholarship (SKOL-ur-ship) money given to a person so that they can attend school

FIND OUT MORE

BOOKS

Blofield, Robert. *How to Make a Movie in 10 Easy Lessons*. Mission Viejo, CA: Walter Foster Publishing, 2015.

Frost, Shelley. *Kids Guide to Movie Making*. New York, NY: Amazon KDP, 2020.

Willoughby, Nick. *Digital Filmmaking for Kids*. Hoboken, NJ: John Wiley & Sons, 2015.

WEBSITES

Black Film Archive: Melvin Van Peebles
https://blackfilmarchive.com/Melvin-Van-Peebles

Britannica: Melvin Van Peebles
https://www.britannica.com/biography/Melvin-Van-Peebles

Criterion Collection: Melvin Van Peebles, Essential Films
https://www.criterion.com/boxsets/4787-melvin-van-peebles-essential-films

INDEX

Blaxploitation films, 16
Brown, Alrick, 19
Chicago, Illinois, 6
critics, film, 12, 18
independent films, 4, 15
New Jack City, 17, 22
Ohio Wesleyan University, 8
Paris, France, 11–13
racism, 14
San Francisco, California, 10
The Story of a Three-Day Pass, 12, 22
Van Peebles, Mario, 4–5, 8–9, 14–15, 17–22

Van Peebles, Melvin
  awards, 12
  childhood, 6–7
  children, 8–9, 15
  college, 7–8
  films, 11–16, 22
  interests, 5, 10–11, 16, 19
  jobs, 8, 10–11
  musicals, 16, 20
  parents, 6
  school, 7, 19
  wife, 9, 11
Watermelon Man, 13, 22

ABOUT THE AUTHORS

Joyce Markovics has written hundreds of books for kids. Movies have helped shaped her outlook on life and inspired her to tell stories. She's grateful to all people who have beaten the odds to make great art. Joyce and Alrick would like to thank Terry John for his contribution to this book.

Alrick A. Brown is a storyteller and an Assistant Professor at NYU who uses filmmaking to touch the hearts and challenge the minds of his audiences. His creativity is shaped by his time living and working in West Africa, his upbringing in New Jersey, and his travels around the world.